Liquid Gold Tattooed

A Collection of Poetry

by Kyoko W.P.

Copyright © Kyoko W.P. , 2023

Book Cover Design by Kyoko W.P.
All rights reserved. No part of this book may be reproduced in any form or by any electronic or mechanical means, including information storage and retrieval systems, without the permission in writing from the publisher, except by a reviewer who may quote brief passages in a review.

Liquid Gold Tattooed   *Poetry*   Kyoko W.P.

Kintsugi, also known as kintsukuroi, is the Japanese art of repairing broken pottery by mending the areas of breakage with lacquer dusted or mixed with powdered gold, silver, or platinum; the method is similar to the maki-e technique. As a philosophy, it treats breakage and repair as part of the history of an object, rather than something to disguise.

Liquid Gold Tattooed | Poetry | **Kyoko W.P.**

Dedication

To all battles and wounds I've survived…
Thank you for allowing me to see that there has always been a **warrior** inside of me.

"The true warrior isn't immune to fear. She fights in spite of it. "–
Francesca Lia Block

"I survived because the fire inside of me burned brighter than the fire around me." - **Joshua Graham**

"You are fierce. You're a survivor. You're a fighter through and through. Little brave, breathe. There is a warrior within you"-. **Beau Taplin**

"I now see how owning our story and loving ourselves through that process is the bravest thing that we will ever do"—**Brené Brown**

"You are a survivor setting the world on fire with your truth. And you never know who needs your light, your warmth, and raging courage." - **Alex Elle**

And to my love, my babies and my sweet, sweet cat Theodore.

Table of Contents:

Find Me in a Poem: pg. 13
In the heart, the home

A Punch to the Gut: pg. 47
My mental maladies
They formed from tragedies

You Kiss me Where it Stings: pg. 83
It's Rare, Raw, Real, Love

Fist Full Of Fortitude: pg. 117
Warrior

Find Me in a Poem:
In the heart, the home

Liquid Gold Tattooed   Poetry   **Kyoko W.P.**

Feelings

Foolishly frightened
Forgetting feelings
are not
facts

My Dear Baby Girls,

Sometimes I sit and cry
about the sweetness that goes by
in the blink of an eye
I was just singing you rock a bye
Oh what id give for that high
Of seeing that precious innocent smile

With Gold

I am, but a sensitive soul
Living in a world of fear and control
Feeling every motion push and pull
Lately, it feels, it's taken a toll
I can feel myself start to unravel; unroll
But I won't grow cold

Oh, no My cracks are filled with gold

Little girl

Little girl, little girl
Why do you cry?
You're far too young to know such pain
But it's all I see in your eyes
Little girl, little girl
You don't have to tell me who or why
You don't have to be okay
You just have to try

Little girl, little girl
I see the fear in your eyes
You need not be afraid
I will sing you lullabies
and hold you under the nights shade

Little girl, little girl,
Don't grow so fast…
Sometimes the world
can feel chaotic,
hard to find your place
Take your time…
find your pace
Don't lose your firefly,
dreams and wishes
Send them way up high
Do it your own way
Light up the sky

Little girl, little girl
Keep your chin up
Don't cry
Inside every little girl,
Is a warrior… with **fire in her eye**

My Hope

I hope you love
yourself one day
The way I love
you
And that you see
yourself
i hope you love
yourself one day
The way I love
you
And that you see
yourself in every
ray of sunshine
The way I see you
I hope you know
the way you
shine,
Is like the moon
Big and bright
and no one could
take that light,
The way
I know
you do

With Grace

What if I decide,
not to be afraid…
But to embrace
the adventure
with grace,
not fear
on my
face

Stillness

Standing in stillness
I observe the world
Spiral around me
Faster and faster
I behold life moving
I'm just a witness
Motion sickness
Hit me with a quickness
But I'm still …
standing in the stillness

A Hug

A safe place
A warm and fuzzy embrace
A tight squeeze
An oxytocin release
A sense of belonging
Feeling the sun dawning
Arms around each other
Sheltered in one another
My mood lifts
Feelings shift
The bond of intimacy
Clasped tightly
Clinging firmly
Close together
Our souls tethered
Hearts beating as one
For a moment, the world stops
It is nurturing, calm
The feeling lingers on

A hug

What If?

Trapped among lives both past and present
Feeling, two separate lives, presence
Experiencing one when I'm asleep
Feeling enough to make me weep
Having flashbacks when I'm awake to what I dreamt
Dreams lingering where they're not meant
One dream like this can feel like several weeks, months even
It's hard to tell, not always a season
I've lived through heart break and sorrow
While awake and while dreaming for tomorrow
But how do these lives coexist?
How do I live like this?
How do I know what's real and what's not?
What if I …
Have reality flip flopped?

One More Hug

If I could
I'd give you
one more hug
A big warm squeeze
As I fit between
Your arms safely
wrapped around me
I'd hold on
as long as I could
I wouldn't let you go
Even though I should
If I could just
give you
one more hug
Just one more
little ounce
of love

It's up to You

I'll make you
a home

Inside of
a poem

It's up to you
which way
the words roam
.

I wish

I wish I could say
I won't let anything hurt you
But I can't
I wish I could say
I won't let your heart break
But I'd be wrong
I wish I could take away your pain
And feel it all just the same
But it's just a wish

Dear Dad

Do I make you proud?
I'm not the seedling
you once knew
Have I bloomed?
I know I need more watering
More time to grow and improve

Time to spend in the sun
My blooming has just begun
But soon I believe it's promising
I'll have the most
Captivating blossoming

Rhythm and Rhyme

Poetry speaks to me
In a way so eloquently
The words paint what you can't see
As they pour out of my memory
A masterpiece in the making
There will be no regret or forsaking
In my rhythm & rhyme making
Because to me,
it's breathtaking

Art of the Poem

Meet me in a poem
Somewhere between the lines
Where the rhythm roams…
Find me in a verse
Don't get lost in the rhymes
Or repetition heard…
Look for me where
emotion evoked phrases exist
Locate me where
expression and imagery persist…
Encounter me
In the heart, the home
Feel me
In the art of the poem

Nature Sings

Mingle with the soil
Tether me to the ground
Take me away from the turmoil
I just want to hear the sound
That nature sings and surrounds you in
This is where all life began

Disability

I miss driving
& it's independence.
I miss walking without a Walker
or assistance.
I miss dancing around
without the fear of collapsing.
I miss friends & seeing people.
No one visits, no one's asking.
But I suppose in actuality
it's really not that bad
It's just sometimes,
I feel overwhelmingly sad

Pain

Pain can have you praying "please!!"
Crying on your knees
Letting out your wildest screams
Make you see unreal things
Erase large amounts of memories
Or even force you to feel every part of your body
But it can also bring new songs to sing
New creating,
new beings
& new beginnings
Pain is something
you deal with or you don't
But if you think it will just go away
It won't

Old Wounds

Old wounds
can bleed
new blood
They don't
always heal

Old wounds
can bring the bad
they remind us of
But they, are also
reminders
to feel

A Single Tear Drop

a single tear drop
is a minuscule
fragment of affliction …
its a speck of vast emotions
all encapsulated
in one single splash…
imagine the pain that remains in the tears not cried
but put a side
to hide

The Morning Wait

It's peaceful
It's calm
But she is not
But for a few short moments
The chaos is forgot
We wait while the sun rises
Peeking from the cloud disguises
The world is still
Birds still sleeping
Leaves move slowly with the breeze
The morning wait puts my soul at ease

Lost Little Girl

I can find myself in words on paper
Each verse another layer
Discovering with each new line
Maybe in a riddle or rhyme
But somewhere within this journal
Are still just the feelings of a lost little girl

Some Days

Some days I'm okay
But today is not some days
And then when it turns night
That's when my brain likes to play
Tricks on me
and my memory
Darkness creeps in every crevice
Tainting everything
that is precious
You'd think I'd learn some lessons
But I just need more sessions
Of Therapy
Maybe I'll find some clarity
Find some familiarity
Because primarily
This will only last temporarily
And soon
I'll be sitting in my serenity

Okay

The pain fades..
But
Some days it rains.
And when it rains
The pain
Emerges in spades
And all you can do is wait.
No matter how much it frustrates...
You
You can take the time to create
I know the sun can be hard to locate.
But I promise.
It
Will
Be
Okay

Reality

What if all of my life has been a dream

and all my dreams…

reality?

Blanket

Like a cloudy day,
A shield from the world
outside.
It's a blanket of peace
and comfort
A giant blanket fort
I could spend forever in
Hiding in the dark,
shades of Gray

Forgotten

Sometimes I feel invisible
Did I just disappear
I scream and I yell
But no one can hear
And then I wonder
Am I still here?
I feel forgotten
Like I don't exist
I fight to be seen
I try, I persist
Am I slowly drifting away
Do you no longer see my heart
Right here on display?

Keep my Heart Alive

Maybe I dance to the beat of my own drummer.. or
Maybe I am the drummer
Still looking for my beat
I feel it as it changes right under my feet

Maybe I sing to my own melody
Lost in the rhythm of life
And it's swift changing keys
They can be sharp, haunting
Full of melancholy

I'm lost in the lyrics
that stimulate my mind
But there are moments of clarity
Where the words just unwind
Those moments of solace
 Happen time to time

										Those are the times
									That keep my heart alive

I Wasn't Ready

Do you think he would even recognize me?
So much has changed
It's been nearly two decades since I saw his face
Two decades of waves of grief with very little grace
I miss him every day
I wonder what he'd think of me now
I wonder what he'd say
Am I making him proud?
Or did I lose my way
I'm not the person I used to be
Not before he passed away
I wasn't ready
I lost him nine days before my 14th birthday…
I still have so much left to say

Emotional Storm

After the storm,
There's a stillness to the air
A chaotic calmness resonating
A weathered warmth
and hostile hush

Shatter

And the biggest thing that broke my heart
Was watching yours shatter
I tried to keep the pieces together
But it didn't really matter
The damage was done
My oath to protect you,
Broken
I never wanted any of this for you
To have your heart break open

If I could fix it with my words,
well they'd already been spoken

Bad Dream

Chaos and cancer
War and disaster
Make it go faster
Feel frozen in a bad dream
Is everything as bad as it seems?
What does any of this even mean?
I don't know, but it's breaking my heart
Come take a look,
it's falling apart

A Punch to the Gut:
My mental maladies
They formed from tragedies

Liquid Gold Tattooed   *Poetry*   **Kyoko W.P.**

The Prelude

Been beaten and bruised
Blamed and accused
Turned away and refused
Felt empty and used
Lost and confused
Utterly disapproved
But allow me to be excused
I'm no longer consumed
That was just the prelude
Because I have cocooned
Through metamorphosis,
I have been improved

Return to Hell

Why do you keep coming back
Night after night like that?
Why can't you grant this peace
And let me rest while I sleep.
It's been years and I can still hear you yell
Whenever I dream, I return to that hell
Like I'm dropped right back into my old life
Living the role again as your meek little wife
I'm aware it's not right and that I'm not awake
I'm just trying to figure out and plot my escape
Sometimes I'm stuck in that life for months because of the dreams pacing
But whenever I do wake up, I feel panicked, sweating..

My heart racing

Won't See You Again

The fog has lifted
My spirit shifted
I once was gifted
But now I don't know,
how
to talk to you

Cause it was easier then
Back when
We were younger with discipline
stronger voice within

And now the story's old
Nothing left to be told
I'm getting on the road
Won't see you again

So this it then
It's been real friend

Under your Pillow

Keep a knife, under your pillow, as you sleep…
For thats when the monsters tend to creep
They send their demons to torture; to reap
You reap what you sow, is what they say…
Be careful each day, be prepared to pay
As you sleep, under your pillow, keep a knife
It may be the one thing to save your life

Curated Catastrophe

Diffuse the IED of dishonesty
Before we all combust from the blow you fraudulently
handled as love for me
But now I see
This disaster was always meant to be
It didn't matter what I tried to be
Or all the love you quickly stole from me
This was always meant to be…
A tragedy

Silence

Your silence sends
sound waves screeching
more resounding
than your
screams
ever could

My Mental Maladies

My mental maladies
They formed from tragedies;
Moments that happened with me
Fragments of what could be
Particles of things once believed
But there's nothing wrong in me
/for you to decide/
Nothing for you to see
For what once was catastrophe
is no longer masquerading,
like a moving masterpiece;
I'm constantly translating
/nothing to hide/

Pardon Me

strength with an iron will
doesn't make this pill
any easier to swallow
down, even with water
it's still stuck in the gut
-ter of my thoughts
that I can't wash out
so pardon me,
while I scream and shout
this is not what I want

How Does It Feel

Waking up crying
Feeling empty in my heart
We were so connected
Now we feel two worlds apart
A pain in the gut
I can't ignore
Tell me, how does it feel
to not love me anymore?

Once Was War

Just like all the debris,
left from the storm.
It's up to you
to clear that path,
and make a way-
where there once
was war.

Tenacity

Time to cut ties with the tastes of tired twisted truths in tempting tones
Tortured and tainted by the thieves toxicity that tip toe through thoughts
Terrorizing threats of tragedy tumble in like tides with theatrics
Tattering taunted tepid tears
touched by travesty and tension
Thoughts trapped that terrify
Triggers tapped that terrorize
Tread through the trauma and terrifying tragedy
Tactfully tying together the tangled tattered twists, turns and timing

Tenacity takes time to thrive

Abyss

I'm screaming out
my lungs to you
Somehow
you can't hear me
I'm yelling
into the abyss

Is there anyone
besides me

One Moment

One moment
One friend
One phone call
One doorbell
One knock
Between you
and finding out
your entire life is changed
your heart shattered
Trying to rearrange
The pattern

One phone call
One doorbell
One knock
One friend
Between you and finding out
it's all come to an end

One bell
One knock
One call
Between you and the moment
you started to fall

One bell
One knock
Between you and the moment
you felt the clock stop

One bell
Between blissful ignorance
and it all going to hell

It only takes one moment

Break

I can break
I can break and mend
Push me so far until I bend
over backwards till it ends

Does it end?

Predator

It doesn't matter
how many years have passed
I can still feel you choke me
I can still feel your grasp
your grabs and your grip
Fighting my screams
by biting my lip
You tossed and threw me
like rag doll
You behaved like a predator
ready to maul
I closed my eyes until it was over
The shame and the pain,
the full – body exposure
I'll never forget
but I'll always long for
closure

It Wasn't Love

Have you ever had your heart break?
You could hear it shatter
 Into pieces of what should've been
Torn and tattered matter of shreds of what could've been
The bruises and batter bestowed upon me
It wasn't love
It was all you

Perfect Crime

You think you got away clean
And you leave the scene
But there's no such thing
As a perfect crime
Someone is left hurting every time
… No such thing as a perfect crime

Holding Onto the Heaven we had once

Suffocating in sadness
from this
malicious madness
How one
Could be so carefully callus
Such crafted cruelty
Executing exactness
Fabricated in Philosophies
you spew as prophesies
Here I am hurt and hopeless,
hastily holding onto the heaven, we had once

The Wrong One

No matter what
you will always find fault
Fault in anything
I do or have done
You never once give me the benefit of doubt
You've already decided
I was the wrong one

You Left

You left to start a new life
A new baby, a new wife
You left behind the three girls you had
You left them broken, with no more dad
You left behind the shattered shards
You left me to mend three broken hearts
You left the ones you claimed to love
You left more damage than I could conceive of

Sting

The tears sting my cheek
where my face hit the floor
Collapsed in defeat
I don't want to live

like this anymore

I'm the one

Try as I may
I could never display
How much I was betrayed
In such a way
That almost put me in a grave
But there's things you can't change
Like the way you behaved
The mountains you caved
The games that you played
The emotions you disarrayed
The haunting memories you made
You had all your plans laid
But I'm the one
I'm the one that paid

Never

You never call
When you say you will

You never see me
But you promise you will

You don't love me
But I love you still

Melancholy Musical

I'm frozen and time stops
I can count my tear drops
They start to form a melody
As they form and fall from me
They drip and dance across my cheeks
And tell a tale my words can't speak
They have their own melancholy musical
While I'm powerless and scream within my soul
They find their way off my face
In patterns that I can trace
And because I am paralyzed
I bear witness to the ballet before my eyes

Anxious

I can't even take this
I don't have the patience
I'm nervous and anxious
My chest feels tight
where it once felt spacious

Worthless

Am I
Worthless?

My just brain keeps repeating
"You deserve this!"

And I'm starting to believe it's true
When your mind is a battlefield
It's a little hard not to do

But I'm not worthless
There's just trauma I can't undo

You might feel the same
If it happened to you

No Big Deal

I just want
you to know
How much
you make me
feel
Like you could just,
Toss me a side
No worry,
no big deal

The Beast

You drink my torment
Like red wine

Devour my pain
Like grapes from a vine

When will enough hurt
Quench your thirst
I thought it was love
But it was more like curse

I will no longer allow myself to be your feast
I guess I was your beauty
And you were truly a beast

Enough

I'll never be enough to be the one
I'll never be enough to your sun

I'll never be enough to win your heart
I'll never be enough to love like art

I'll never be enough to be shown grace
I'll never be enough to wear white lace

I'll never be enough for you
I'll never be enough

Alice

A punch to the gut
And a slap in the face
Each step, which I can't retrace
How did I get here
Living within fear
Caged in the chaos
Almost saw my life lost
But at what cost
I'm free to fly now
But sometimes still forget how
I can be brave and face the day
Or I can crumble and hideaway
I didn't lose my life
But I lost my balance
It's like I'm in wonderland
Please, call me Alice

Petals

You picked my petals.
One
by
One.
And I let you,
thinking... I had won.
Truth be told,
before you finished with my petals...
You were already
done.

Reduced to Nothing

A flicker, a flash , a flame
A blaze of fire ignites inside
It scorches with a fierce torch
Embracing the warmth of it while it sears
Melting
Watch as it all goes up in smoke
Smoldering
Reduced to nothing
but ashes
and char

Whats Remained

So I'm here
Can't go back
Can only be present
Can only move forward

(What is it that you're moving toward?)

To be clear
I'm closing the chapter
on the past
Quicker than a slammed door would

There's nothing left there
It can't be changed
I stay in the now
I didn't get here, unscathed
But it's my life, I saved
In my tears, I bathed
Blamed and shamed
I am whats remained

Losing you

The decisions been made
It's very clear
Lay me down in my grave
You won't shed one tear
Leave me here, afraid
Because losing you
is my biggest fear

You Kiss me Where it Stings:

It's Rare, Raw, Real, Love

Liquid Gold Tattooed   *Poetry*   **Kyoko W.P.**

Your Souls Engraving

I've always craved a sense of belonging,
Never felt I was one to fit in
Always trying, always fawning
But then I met you, goose bumps on my skin
It was you I had been craving,
It is you, whom I belong
Your souls engraving,
On my Soul, like a melodic love song

Golden Dust

All in a golden afternoon,
under the skies of cloudless blue
I see your face, feel your warmth & reach out to you
Eyes are sparkling from the sun shining down
There's an enchanting sparkle, glistening, all around
Enriched with magnificent golden dust
Natures beauty surrounding us

Tender Love

Your love is something new,
So tender
My body had no choice but to completely surrender
Itself
To You
It's like nothing in my life
I've ever felt
So I'll stay here in this moment
And melt
Away
With you

Like you

I did not find you first
But I looked and I searched
And somehow I found you
in this immense universe
The skies turned black
Your eyes so blue
Of all
the stars shining
None shine
quite like you
I may not have been
a part of your past
But I wish
to always
be your
last

The Warmest Touch

This air is cold
And still I melt
You've got the warmest touch
I've ever felt …

In my entire life

Intoxicating High

I never grow tired

the scent of your skin
An intoxicating high

the moment it hits
With every inhale,

gently brighter
You make my soul

feel a little bit lighter

Like this

I'm here now
It's time to look around
To look and see
The Earth, the ground
Look up and see
The stars i missed
Feel the air,
Taste the mist
that kiss my lips
Life, is for moments,
under the moon
..like this

It's Rare, Raw, Real, Love

It is glowing,
Can't you see?
It's singing,
Can't you hear…
It's melody?
Doesn't it smell
…heavenly?

It is love.
It's rare, raw, real, love.

All I Can See is You

                           I read you
                          line by line
                        Even the ones
                     that send shivers
                        up my spine
                          I see you
                       in the spaces
                          Can feel
                    your heartbeat
                 as the pace races
                      I can find you
                    on blank pages
                      Like theaters
                      set up stages
                    Those places
                     soon fill up
                    with phrases
                   All I can see
                         is you
                      where the
                        page is

Captivating

Everything is so hazy
I can hardly see
Everything is moving like
Lights on a rainy street blazing
All I can see is you
And you are all that I'm craving
The twinkle in your eye,
Its captivating
Your eyes gaze at me,
My heart palpitating
Two souls,
…embracing

The Fog

The fog is thick and dense
Of what's in front,
You can't make sense
Yet I still reach for your touch
Even when I can't see much

But I can still feel you
And I can still see you

The fog is lifting now
Things getting clearer out
I can finally see your face
All the fog has begun to break

I can feel you
I can see you

Through the dense air
See your wavy hair
I'd walk blindly to get to you

But it was clear
And you were near
To feel you,
There's nothing I wouldn't do

Yes the airs been thick
But we're always quick
To find our ways

And I can see you

And I can feel you

Because of You

I saw clearly
for the first time that day.

That was the day
everything had changed.
My whole life rearranged.

The way you looked at me
as I played with my hair
We couldn't deny the energy
in the atmosphere

In the blink of an eye,
I fell in love

You showed me
what stars are made of
And to dance
floating under the moon

I believe in love
because of you

Burns like Dying Stars

My skin burns
like dying stars
Every time
you touch
my scars
But even with
skin peeling
I can feel
the wounds healing

Yin & Yang

You love me
where it hurts
You kiss me
where it stings
Your scent is like an anesthesia for the soul
With all the calm
it brings
My heart
no longer chaotic and out of control
Now my heart
sings

         To my Yang
         I found my Yin

Chosen

I'd cross
Every ocean
Every wave
Every motion
To show
My devotion
I'd cut my heart open
Expose all emotion
Because my soul
Has spoken
It's you
It has chosen

You're My Him

Here I am
In your arms again
You opened up
You let me in
You took a dip
But now you swim
You kiss me once
And I kiss you ten
I'm your
her
And you're
my him

It Was Automatic

You're like magic.
You found me when my life was tragic
A mess of tears, panic
& manic
Admist my most dramatic
Going through something traumatic
And you knew how to fix it
Like a mechanic
It was automatic
We were friends, it was organic
But that grew into something romantic
A tranquil and serene dynamic
I knew from day one,
I could feel the static
When our souls met
It was climatic

Heartbeat Song

I want to melt
into your chest
As I drown
to the song
of your heartbeat
And inhale your scent
as it sweeps
me
off my feet
I want to stay right here,
Drift off to sleep
With your song
playing
on repeat

What would it take to make you mine?

What would it take to
make you mine?
I want to hold you all the
time
Be the glimmer in your
eyes
What would it take to
make you realize
When you're around I'm
full of butterflies
On cloud nine as it
glides through the sky
The magic I feel when
our souls collide
When I'm with you I
have nothing to hide
What would it take to
make you mine?

I Didn't Believe

You are the poetry
I didn't know I could write.

The words
I never knew I could feel.

And the experience
I didn't believe
was real.

Indefinitely

Take my hand,
Would you follow me?
I get terribly lost.
I wouldn't know where to lead.
But I promise to love you,

Indefinitely.

I Can See the Moon Glisten

Crystal turquoise blue
Like the ocean
Warm waves pull me in
I won't drown,
I dive within
The waters calm
I know I can swim

You have the gentlest eyes
I've ever been in

Lady of the Sea

Like an anchor
You keep me grounded
Like the waves
You roll with me
And like a light house you help me through the dark

I am your lady of the sea
Wherever you are,
I want to be

Love

I don't know
what i knew
but it wasn't love
until it was ...

you

Sweet Simple Melody

It beats;
bouncing bombastically
between each breath,
I breathe
It radiates;
Pulsating in my palms between each squeeze
Two hearts
One song
They're meant to be...
One sweet simple melody

What Are We

What is the heart
 If not pounding

What is love
If not astounding

What is life
If not in your surrounding

What are we
If not the tune that keeps sounding

Remember

Remember the orange halls
Remember the work calls
When we were only a few feet away

Remember the deep talks
Remember the long walks
And any chance we got to play

Remember the love born
Remember the walls torn
And how your chest is where I lay

There are just so many words
It's impossible to even say what I want to say

But I know I want to be with you everyday

Wherever You are I Want to be too

My soul knew you were the one
Long before my brain caught on

I could feel it
Something was different
The unexpected experience of
The energy
The intensity
And then the obvious
Burst of clarity
Of what was right in front of me

What we have is rare
Souls long to find their mates
But I found mine in you

It's us against the world
I promise
It's true
Wherever you are
I want to be too

Synchronized Beating

My heart is pounding
My brain is reeling
Could it be possible
It's love I'm feeling?

I feel us floating
The stars; our ceiling
Two hearts in rhythm
Synchronized beating

Blind

It's so pure, this love.
What every girl dreams of…
I never believed enough
 to dream it
Now that I have it
I don't want ever to leave it

It's so pure, this love.
It's organic.
This love flows like water.
The water drifts and bends
to where our souls begin.

I've been blind for so long
Now, everything is new
I opened my eyes for the first time
the day I realized I loved you.

In the End

I'd walk through that
hellacious hall of horrors
again
If it promised
the heaven I have with him
in the end

Fist Full Of Fortitude:
Warrior

Warrior

There's a warrior inside
of me
She gets me where I
need to be
She slays dragons and
fights monsters
All the horrific things
that haunt her
She is stronger than you
could fathom
She finds grounding
where she lands on
She sings songs that
soothe the soul
when the world around
her begins to unravel
She's always been able to
piece things back where
they need to be
She's always been braver
than any could see
The warrior inside of me
... I am she
and she is me

I'm Still Here

I have evolved stronger
by facing my fears
I watered these seeds
with my abundant tears
Blooming back to life
after poisoned years
I'm still here

Her Love

Despite the constant rain and thunder
She can still find a way to smile under
All those broken pieces

Her love never ceases

Behind the Words you Read

I am the mess behind the words that you read
The one that looks distressed as you see my scars bleed
The one facing the demons that only I can see
Feeling every evil being surrounding me
The one who must deal with all of this inside of me
And now the one no longer who she used to be
Not after having nearly everything taken from me
I am this way because of what has happened to me
But if nothing else it only further enhanced my empathy
You will not get to make darkness out of me
I am the one who will always love compassionately
The one who's light cannot be dimmed, you see
 This light, it shines infinitely

Still Bloom

Even in the darkest of nights,
A flower can still **bloom**.

Still Standing

I am like a tree,
at the end of autumn.
The branches,
like my bones,
are bare,
exposed and vulnerable
But still standing
And despite the cold,
and blows of gust
I'm still standing
……. I am strong

A Soul full of Sorrow

There's a raging
sea of emotions
Inside of me

And when they come to shore
With waves of complication
I'm still thankful

She may cry tears
That fill a sea
She still finds a reason to hope

She may crack and bend
But she never breaks
Not completely

A soul of sorrow
But the armor
Of a warrior

Balance

Balance is something
I can't always keep
No matter the surface
It always feels steep
I can feel the floor moving
From right beneath me
Everything is so blurry,
Surrounding
My legs start to wobble
and shake
My senses are unstable
Nauseating headache
I have no stamina
Might need a medical examiner
My physique is weak
I can barely speak
I may be frail and fragile in
my physical body

But my spirit is full of ferocious strength
inside of me
I may stumble, fall
or faint
Spill on the floor
Like liquid paint
Increased heart rate
But I always get back up and stand
Even if I don't always land

My Light

Maybe it's not that my light
doesn't shine bright enough
for others to care,
Maybe it's that my light shines too bright;
hard to witness, to bear.
So the world throws its shade and its filters,
in forms of trauma and tragedy,
in attempts to dim or dull
my light capacity.
But I still glow and gleam in the dark…
Beaming dazzling light into the night sky,
like art

Brilliant Flame

A tattoo that can't be erased
Your fingers go over them and trace
The pain that remains and shames
But never have you ever once complained
You touched me with love and never with blame
You set my soul on fire
Like a brilliant flame

Still Beating

Your words cut like a knife
Your voice sends vibrations down my spine
The scent of you sends me in a panic
The look in your eyes lends to a fear I can't
Your presence pains my entire being
You can't hear it, but I'm screaming
At least you left my heart
Still beating

Weight on my Shoulders

Carry pain
Like a bag of rocks over my shoulder
Starting to feel like
I'm holding a boulder
Every day
The heaviness increases
I don't know if
I remember what peace is
If only I could lighten the load

But because I have purpose
I will continue on the road

Count My Blessings

Forged in the fires of adversity
Fabricated in every ailment
Hindered by every expression
And yet I still
Count my blessings

Better Today

Better today than yesterday
But that isn't to say
That I won't stray
I'm growing, changing, healing each day
Keeping the demons at bay
Still there,
But,
Better today than yesterday
My life still in disarray
Try as I may
Can't take the pain away
But,
Better today than yesterday

Piece of Art
(Kintsukuroi)

Every word is a memory
Each a punch in the gut,
a crack in the heart.
But these wounds
somehow craft me
into a new piece of art.

Hair Down

She let her hair down
for the first time in ages
and let out a sigh she'd been holding in
for what seemed like an eternity.
It is done.
Shoulders relaxed.

It's finally over.

Fist Full of Fortitude

She's a fierce fighter
fresh from the flames you fanned
Famished and fatigued
feeding the fear she feels
She ferociously freed herself
She doesn't fall back,
freeze or fawn
She fights while flesh fragrance
forges through the fire
Fist full of fortitude
She doesn't flinch in the fumes
She is female
She won't forget
she fought for her future

Concrete Flowers

Just like a flower blooming
through a concrete
 sidewalk

So do I
through the barriers
before me

Liquid Gold

I don't want to fall to pieces
I don't want to come unglued
I'll keep my breaks and scars bonded:
Liquid gold tattooed
And when the scars begin to bleed
I'll try to think less of you
The gold in place to remind me that,
I
am
free…
That, I have been renewed

A Goddess Doesn't Whisper
She Sings at the Top of Her Lungs

Kyoko W.P.

Liquid Gold Tattooed | Poetry | Kyoko W.P.

Alexa, play Destinys Child Survivor

For Domestic Violence help:

The National Domestic Violence Hotline aids victims of domestic violence 24 hours a day. Hotline advocates assist victims, and anyone calling on their behalf, by providing crisis intervention, safety planning and referrals to local service providers. The hotline receives more than 24,000 calls a month. 800-799-SAFE (7233)

For Mental health Crisis :

Trained crisis workers are available to talk 24 hours a day, 7 days a week. Your confidential and toll-free call goes to the nearest crisis center in the Lifeline national network. These centers provide crisis counseling and mental health referrals. Call or TEXT 988 or chat 988lifeline.org.

Much love, thanks and appreciation for reading and following me on my journey.

For more follow me on Instagram @Kyokothepoet

The rest of the book is for you to write down your thoughts and feelings if you get inspired :)

Liquid Gold Tattooed   *Poetry*   **Kyoko W.P.**

Hi dad! I love you!

Liquid Gold Tattooed | Poetry | Kyoko W.P.

Made in the USA
Columbia, SC
03 May 2023